Look
Up!

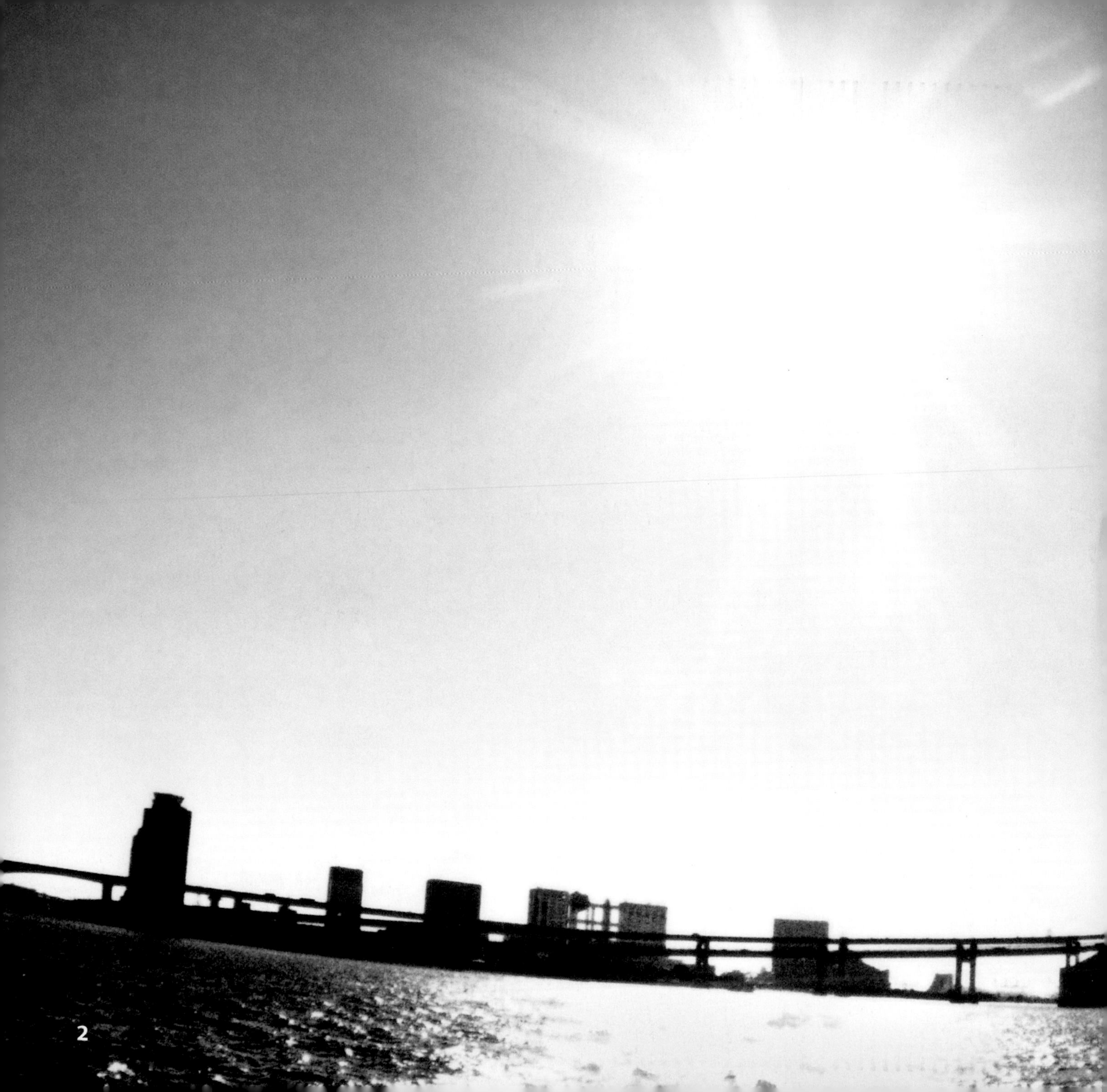

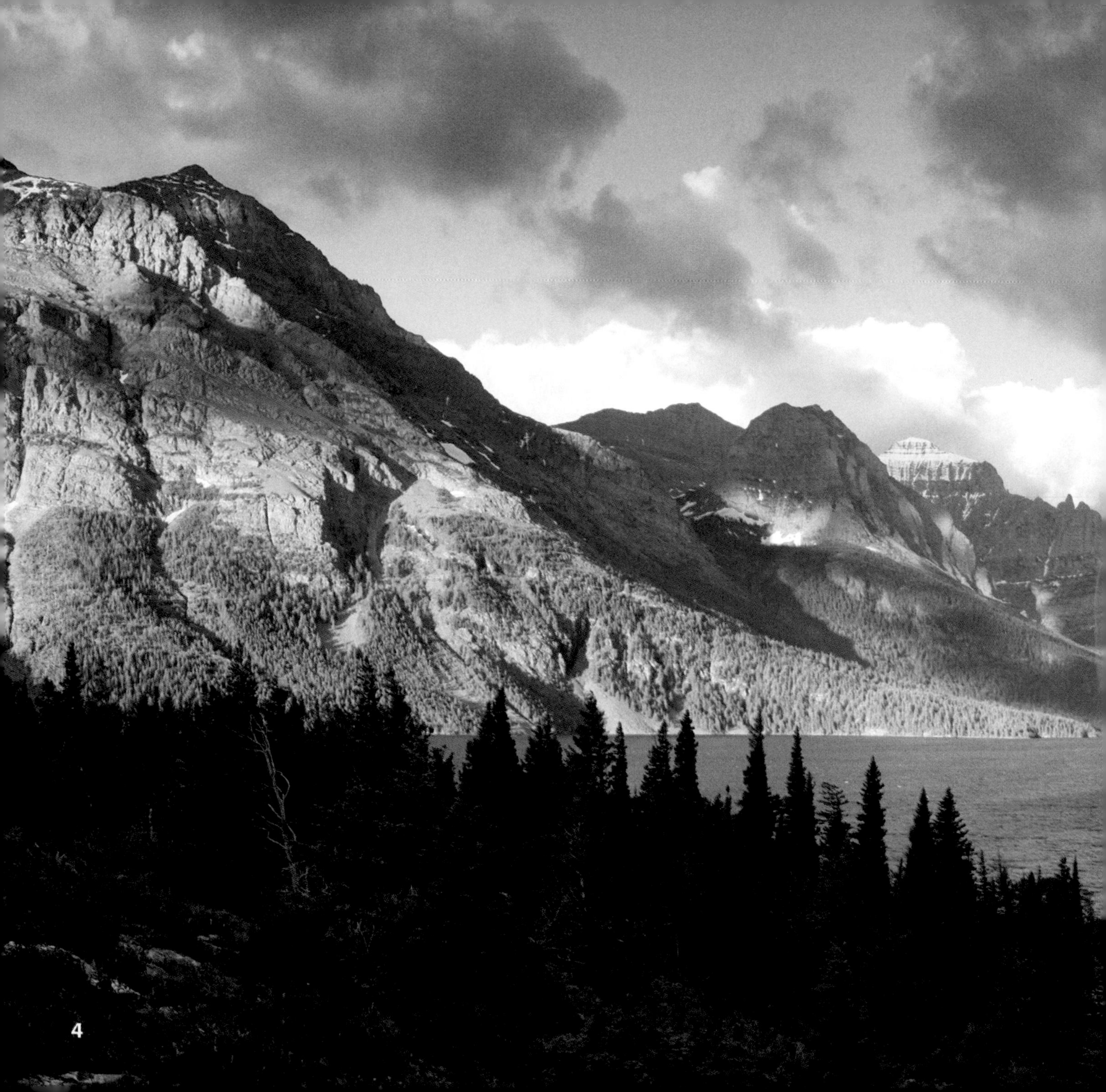

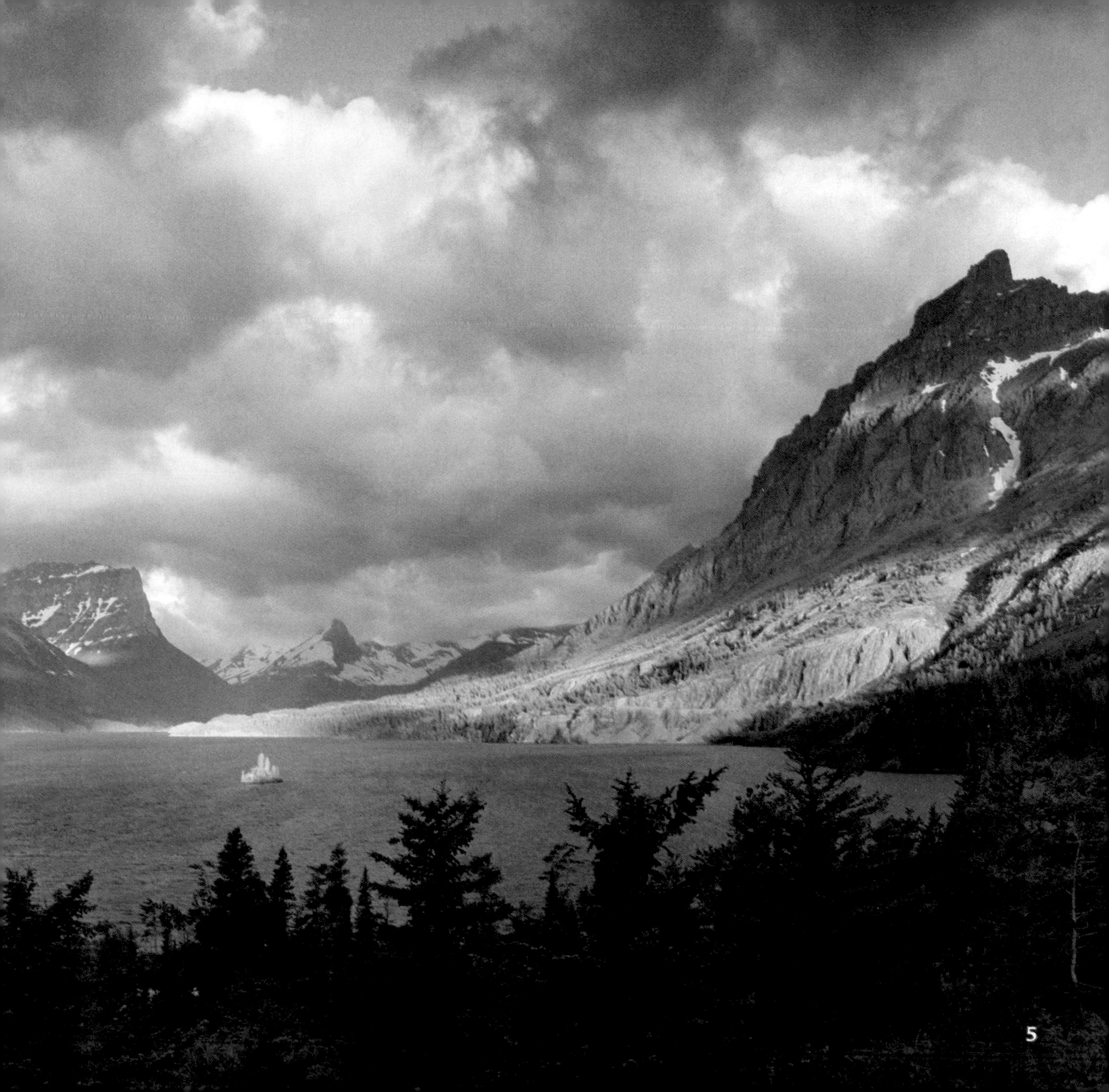

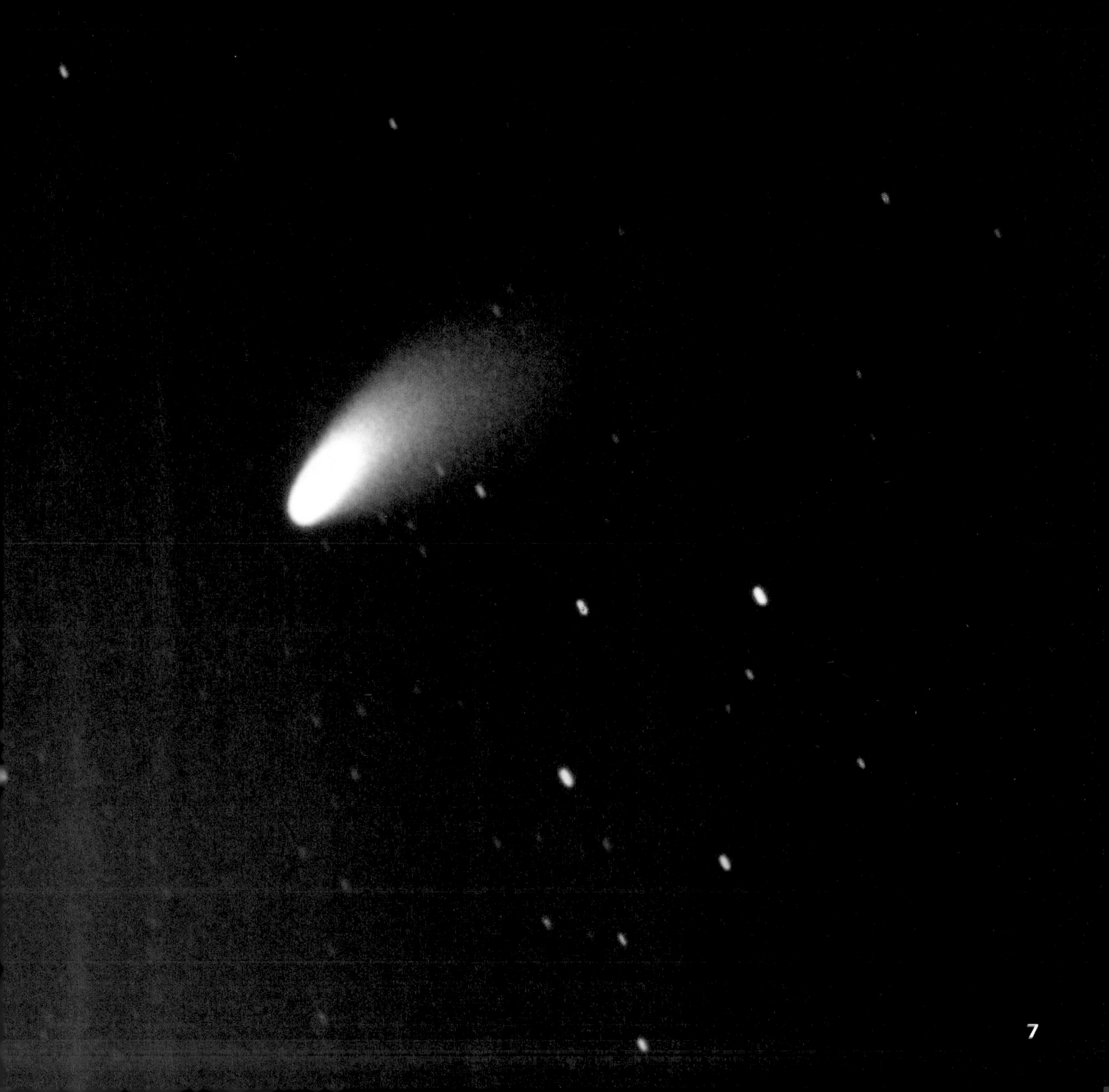

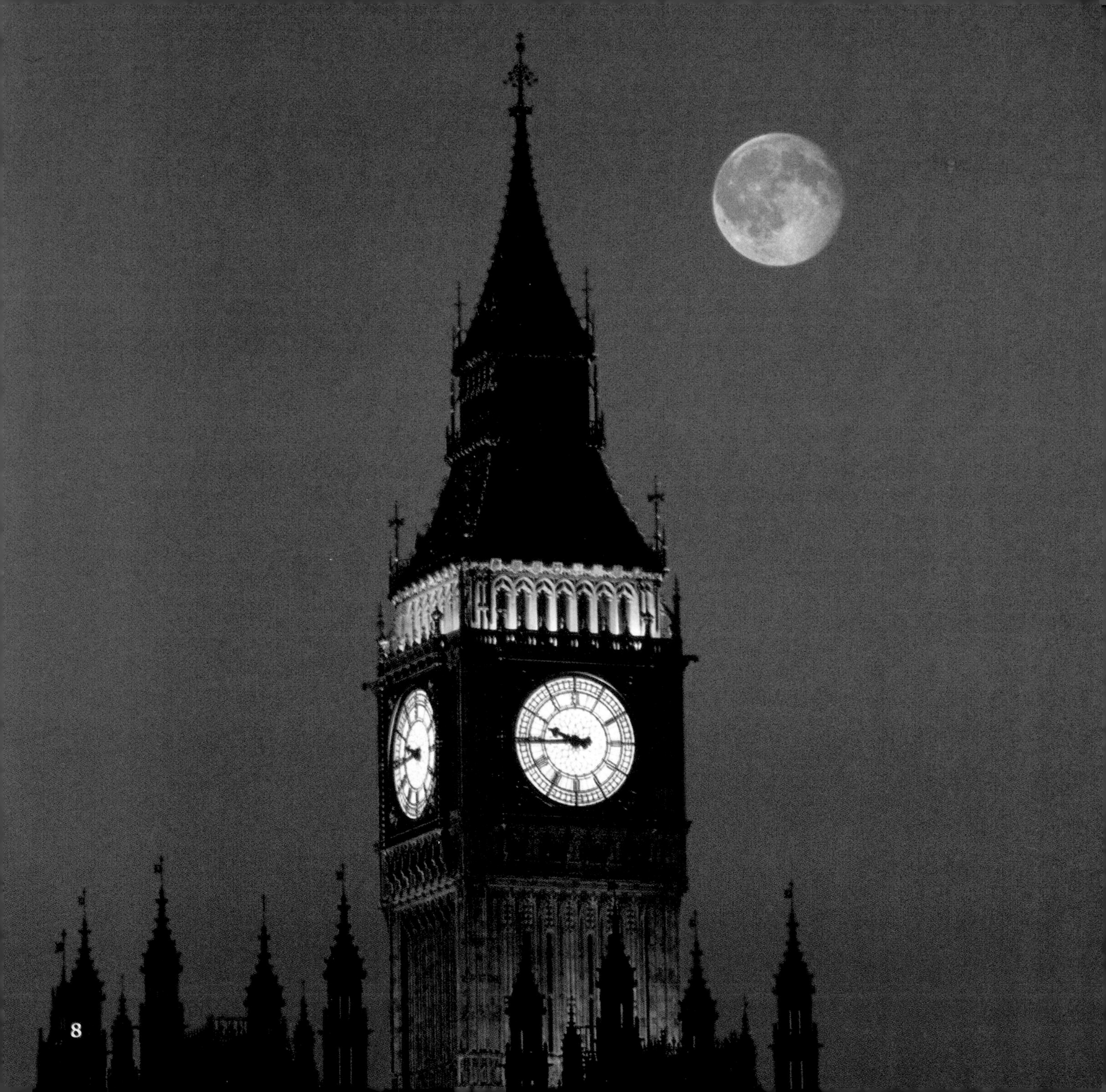